The Black Cockatoo, Finding His Songline

Written and illustrated by Riker Matters

We respect and honour Aboriginal and Torres Strait Islander Elders past, present and future. We acknowledge the stories, traditions and living cultures of Aboriginal and Torres Strait Islander peoples on this land and commit to building a brighter future together.

Library For All Ltd.

Fire crackles.

Wind blows gently.

The children settle around the fire where it is warm, and the night sky is lit by the dancing flames.

"Ash, will you tell us a story?" Lochy asks as he walks over to sit with his cousins.

"Yeah! Just like Granny used to!" exclaims Sara, already cosy, next to her brother Sam.

"PLEASE!" Sam bounces and claps his hands together excitedly.

"OK, I'll tell you about the black cockatoo." Ash smiles at her cousins, the light of the fire warming her face.

Everybody is excited because they love it when Cousin Ash tells stories.

Cousin Ash begins her story...

Way up high, sitting in a gum tree, is a beautiful black cockatoo. His black feathers shine in the morning light. As the sun rises, it catches the red of his tail, blazing brightly.

He stretches his wings and thinks to himself, *I'm going to explore today and see how far I can fly before the sun goes down.*

The black cockatoo opens his wings wide and takes flight.

For a long time, he flies over rivers and hills, until he comes to a place he has not seen before.

He is excited! In this new place, he explores a pile of rocks, a fallen tree and a fresh spring.

Hours pass as he enjoys this new sky. Soon, the day is ending.

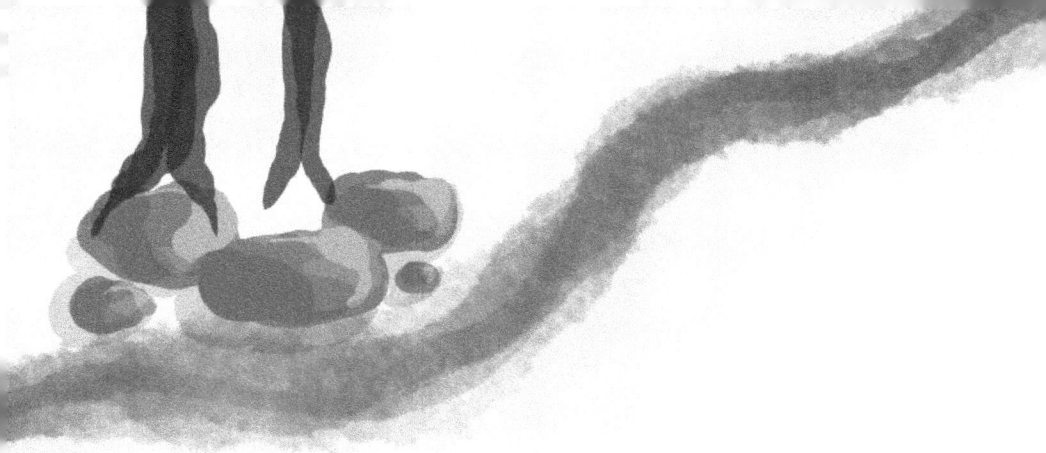

The black cockatoo is ready to fly home, but nothing looks familiar to him. He perches near a river and looks in every direction, but he can't see any landmarks he recognises.

He's a long way from home, but it's okay.

The black cockatoo knows that he can use his instincts to start flying in the right direction. His songline keeps a record. All he must do is remember.

He takes a deep breath, closes his eyes, and sees the path in his mind.

A faint path winds through the bush that he had been exploring.

He follows it back to the places he discovered earlier that day.

A pile of rocks.

A fallen tree.

A fresh spring.

Finally, the black cockatoo comes to a river. He remembers the river. This river was the landmark to find his way home. It was connected to the hills he flew over.

He jumps up and down on the spot, excited that he was able to use his memory to find his way back.

Now his songline has a new journey to record.

Again, the black cockatoo spreads his wings wide and takes off into the sky.

He follows the river, through bushland and towards the hills.

Behind the black cockatoo, the songline grows and grows. It is collecting his story and his happy day of exploration.

He now has new knowledge of the land he lives on, his Country, his home.

As the black cockatoo flies over the hills, he sees in the distance his favourite tree.

He flies towards it because he knows it is a turning point in his journey to get back home.

He looks down and sees a mob of kangaroos settling in by the bushes for the night, some pink galahs noisily perching on a branch, and a snake making a quick dash to the safety of some rocks.

As he turns at his favourite tree, he is greeted by the sight of the great river that marks the place of his home.

He looks for the third bend in the river as he makes his final turn towards home. He sees his home tree come into view, and his family already waiting for him to return.

The black cockatoo flies into his home tree and lands among the flock — his family.

They greet him noisily, as most cockatoos do. He settles into a warm snuggle beside the other black cockatoos.

They ruffle their feathers in anticipation to hear about his exploration today.

The black cockatoo's songline fills the air around him and his family, as they make memories together.

"The end," whispers Cousin Ash. "Now, we should try to go to sleep. It's dark."

"But wait," Sara pipes up. "So, his songline helped him understand where he belonged and how to get home after exploring the Country?"

"And helped him remember his way?" asks Lochy.

"I think he made even more songline," yawns Sam.

"You are all right," says Ash. "We all have our songline too. It shows us where we have been and guides us to where we might go in the future."

"When we go camping next time, I will take you to see Granny's songline paintings and she can tell you more stories about our family songlines."

"Yay!" they all exclaim.

"Now, let's go to bed before Mum comes out!" giggles Ash, quietly putting out the fire.

The cousins sleep soundly, dreaming of their songlines and how they are all connected.

How many stories will your songline collect?

You can use these questions to talk about this book with your family, friends and teachers.

What did you learn from this book?

Describe this book in one word. Funny? Scary? Colourful? Interesting?

How did this book make you feel when you finished reading it?

What was your favourite part of this book?

About the author and illustrator

Riker is a Noongar artist from Perth, Western Australia, with extensive experience in acrylic painting, digital art, illustration and design. Inspiration comes to Riker in all forms; she draws from the Earth, the Ocean, and what connects her emotionally to Country and soul.

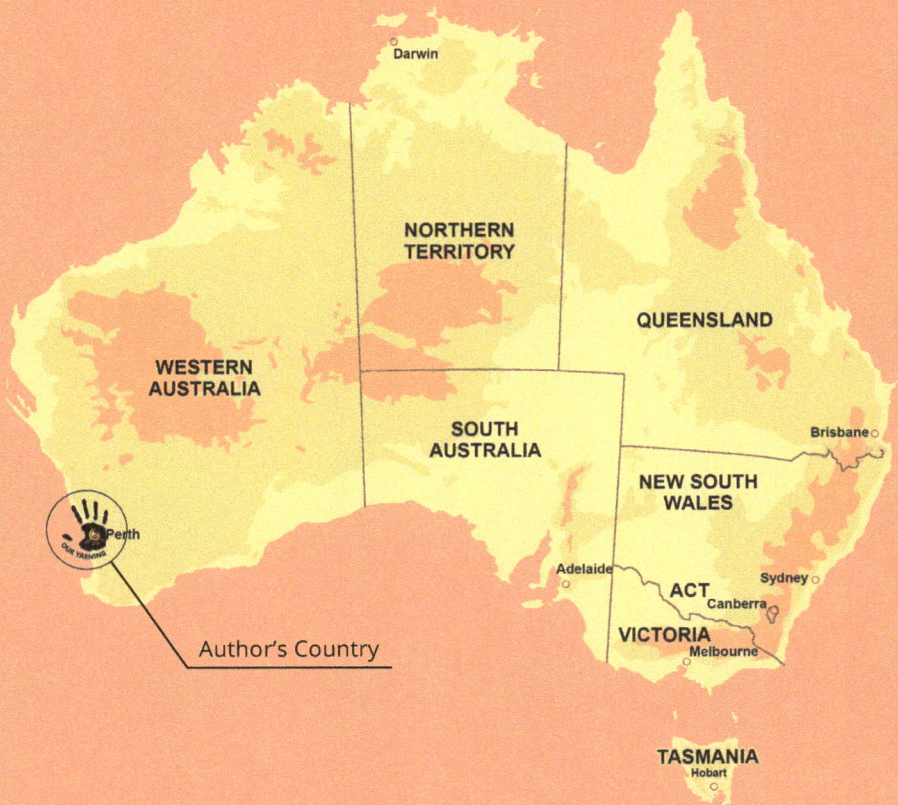

Author's Country

Our Yarning

The Our Yarning collection aligns with the Australian Curriculum through the Cross-Curriculum Priorities — Aboriginal and Torres Strait Islander Histories and Cultures. The collection provides an authentic opportunity for learning and embedding Aboriginal and Torres Strait Islander perspectives because it is written by Aboriginal and Torres Strait Islander people.

We know that children learn better, and enjoy reading more, when they see themselves in the stories, characters and illustrations of the books they read.

To download the app, visit the Google Play Store or Apple Store and search 'Our Yarning'.

libraryforall.org

You're reading Upper Primary

Learner – Beginner readers

Start your reading journey with short words, big ideas and plenty of pictures.

Level 1 – Rising readers

Raise your reading level with more words, simple sentences and exciting images.

Level 2 – Eager readers

Enjoy your reading time with familiar words, but complex sentences.

Level 3 – Progressing readers

Develop your reading skills with creative stories and some challenging vocabulary.

Level 4 – Fluent readers

Step up your reading skills with playful narratives, new words and fun facts.

Middle Primary – Curious readers

Discover your world through science and stories.

Upper Primary – Adventurous readers

Explore your world through science and stories.

The Black Cockatoo, Finding His Songline

First published 2024

Published by Library For All Ltd
Email: info@libraryforall.org
URL: libraryforall.org

Our Yarning logo design by Jason Lee, Bidjipidji Art

Original illustrations by Riker Matters

The Black Cockatoo, Finding His Songline
Matters, Riker
ISBN: 978-1-923339-50-7
SKU04429

www.ingramcontent.com/pod-product-compliance
Lightning Source LLC
Chambersburg PA
CBHW042341040426
42448CB00019B/3363